C000006107

Best Walks
IN THE
PEAK DISTRICT

by Brian Spencer

Bartholomew
An Imprint of HarperCollins*Publishers*

CONTENTS

A Bartholomew Walk Guide
Published by Bartholomew
An Imprint of HarperCollins*Publishers*
77-85 Fulham Palace Road
London W6 8JB

First published 1996
Text © Brian Spencer 1996
Maps © Bartholomew 1996

The walks contained in this guide were
first published in Bartholomew's
Walk the Peak District

Printed in Great Britain by
Scotprint Limited, Musselburgh

ISBN 0 7028 3516 1
96/1/16

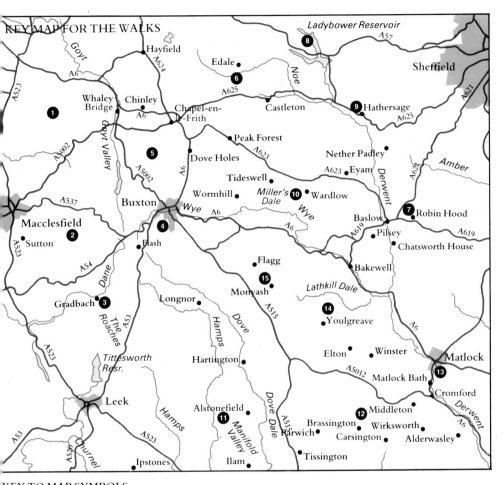

KEY MAP FOR THE WALKS

KEY TO MAP SYMBOLS

————	Main Road	—○—	Railway	⌂	Cairn	*i* Information Centre
———	Minor Road	Ⓐ—	Description of viewpoint	〰	Slope or Crags	▲ʸ ᴴ Youth Hostel
- - - - -	Track and Footpath	〰	Viewpoint		Woods	+ Church or Abbey
– – –	Route of Walk	▲	Summit	P	Parking	∴ Site of Antiquity

INTRODUCTION

1 WALKING IN THE PEAK DISTRICT

When walking in the Peak you can encounter four quite different types of terrain. Probably the easiest walking of all is on the limestone plateau where stone stiles and green lanes indicate the way. In the dales, paths wander through shady woodland and follow bubbling trout rivers. In the north, the unpredictable weather makes navigation across the trackless moors quite difficult. Gritstone edges above the Derwent, or the lower heather moors, are more straightforward and the footpaths are easier to follow.

Walking is a sport which can fulfil the needs of everyone. You can adapt it to suit your own preferences and it is the healthiest of activities. Your inclination might be to walk two or three miles along a gentle track instead of one of the more arduous long distance routes but, whatever the walk, it will always improve your general well-being. Walking should be anything from an individual pastime to a family stroll, or maybe a group of friends enjoying the fresh air and open spaces of our countryside. There is no need for walking to be competitive and, to get the most from walking, it shouldn't be regarded simply as a means of covering a given distance in the shortest possible time.

As with all other outdoor activities, walking is safe provided a few simple common sense rules are followed:

a   Make sure you are fit enough to complete the walk.

b   Always try to let others know where you intend going.

c   Be clothed adequately for the weather and always wear suitable footwear.

d   Always allow plenty of time for the walk, especially if it is longer or harder than you have done before.

e   Whatever the distance you plan to walk, always allow plenty of daylight hours unless you are absolutely certain of the route.

f   If mist or bad weather come on unexpectedly do not panic and try to remember the last certain feature which you have passed (road, farm, wood, etc). Then work out your route from that point on the map but be sure of your route before continuing.

g   Do not dislodge stones on the high edges: there may be climbers or other walkers on the lower crags and slopes.

h   Unfortunately, accidents can happen even on the easiest of walks. If this should be the case and you need the help of others, make sure that the inured person is safe in a place where no further injury is likely to occur. For example, the injured person should not be left on a steep hillside or in danger from falling rocks. If you can not leave anyone with the injured person and, even if they are conscious, try to leave a written note explaining their injuries and whatever you have done in the way of first aid treatment. Make sure you know exactly where you left them and then go to find assistance. If you meet a National Park Ranger, tell him or her what has happened. Otherwise, make your way to a telephone and dial 999 and ask for assistance. Unless the accident has happened within easy access of a road, then it is the responsibility of the Police to arrange evacuation. Always give accurate directions of how to find the casualty and, if possible, give an indication of the injuries involved.

i   When walking in open country, learn to keep an eye on the immediate foreground while you admire the scenery or plan the route ahead. This may sound difficult, especially to a beginner but, once you can adapt to this method, your enjoyment will increase.

j   It's best to walk at a steady pace, always on the flat of the feet as this is less tiring. Try not to walk directly up or downhill. A zig-zag route is a more comfortable way of negotiating a slope. Running directly down hill is a major cause of erosion on popular hillsides.

k   When walking along a country road, walk on the right, facing the traffic. The exception to this rule is, when approaching a blind bend, the walker should cross over to the left and so have a clear view and also be seen in both directions.

l   Finally, always park your car where it will not cause inconvenience to other road users or prevent a farmer from gaining access to his fields. Make sure that you lock your car and hide any valuables before leaving or, preferably, carry all valuables with you.

2 EQUIPMENT

Equipment, including clothing, footwear and rucksacks, is essentially a personal thing and depends on several factors, such as the type of activity planned, the time of year and weather likely to be encountered.

All too often, a novice walker will spend pounds on a fashionable jacket but will skimp when it comes to buying footwear or a comfortable rucksack. Blistered and tired feet quickly remove all enjoyment from even the most exciting walk and a poorly balanced rucksack will soon feel as though it is carrying half a hundredweight. Well designed equipment is not only more comfortable but, being better made, it is longer lasting.

Clothing should be adequate for the day. In summer, remember to protect your head and neck which are particularly vulnerable in a strong sun. Wear light woollen socks and lightweight boots or strong shoes will be adequate. A spare pullover and waterproofs carried in the rucksack should, however, always be there in case you need them.

Winter wear is a much more serious affair. Remember that once the body starts to lose heat it becomes much less efficient. Jeans are particularly unsuitable for winter wear and can sometimes even be downright dangerous.

Waterproof clothing is an area where it pays to buy the best you can afford. Make sure that the jacket is loose-fitting, has a generous hood and comes down at least to knee level. Waterproof overtrousers will not only offer complete protection in the rain but they are also windproof. Do not be misled by flimsy nylon 'showerproof' affairs. Remember, too, that garments made from rubberised or plastic material are heavy to carry and wear and they trap body condensation. Your rucksack should have wide, padded carrying straps for comfort.

It is important to wear boots that fit well or shoes with a good moulded sole – blisters can ruin any walk! Woollen socks are much more comfortable than any other fibre. Your clothes should be comfortable and not likely to catch on twigs and bushes. In winter, it's best to take two lightweight jumpers, one at least with a crew neck. You will find this better than wearing one jumper made of heavy material. Your jacket should have a hood and it should be windproof

and loose enough for an extra layer of warmer clothing underneath. A woollen hat, which can be pulled well down, is essential in winter.

A piece of semi-rigid plastic foam carried in the rucksack makes a handy and yet almost weightless seat for open-air picnics.

An area map, as well as this guide, is useful for accuate navigation and it adds to the enjoyment of a walk. Finally, a small first aid kit is an invaluable help in coping with cuts and other small injuries.

3 PUBLIC RIGHTS OF WAY

Although most of the area covered by this guide comes within the authority of the Peak National Park, this does not mean that there is complete freedom of access to walk anywhere. Much of the land within the park is privately owned and what might appear to be an ideal spot for a picnic, or somewhere to exercise the dog, is often part of another person's livelihood.

In 1949 the *National Parks and Access to the Countryside Act* tidied up the law covering rights of way. Following public consultation, maps were drawn up by the Countryside Authorities of England and Wales to show all the rights of way. Copies of these maps are available for public inspection and are invaluable when trying to resolve doubts over little used footpaths. Once on the map, the right of way is irrefutable.

Right of way means that anyone may walk freely on a defined footpath or ride a horse or pedal cycle along a public bridleway. No-one may interfere with this right and the walker is within his rights if he removes any obstruction along the route, provided that he has not set out purposely with the intention of removing that obstruction. All obstructions should be reported to the local Highways Authority.

Free access to footpaths and bridleways does mean that certain guidelines should be followed as courtesy to those who live and work in the area. For example, you should only sit down to picnic where it does not interfere with other walkers or the landowner. All gates must be closed to prevent stock from straying and dogs must be kept under close control – usually this is interpreted as meaning that they should be kept on a leash. Motor vehicles must not be driven along a public footpath or bridleway without the landowner's consent.

A farmer can put a docile mature beef bull with a herd of cows or heifers, in a field crossed by a public footpath. Beef bulls such as Herefords (usually brown/red colour) are unlikely to be upset by passers-by but dairy bulls, like the black and white Friesian, can be dangerous by nature. It is, therefore, illegal for a farmer to let a dairy bull roam loose in a field open to public access.

Most public rights of way within the Peak National park have been clearly defined and are marked as such on available maps. They are marked on the Ordnance Survey one inch (1:63 360) and metric (1:50 000) maps as red dots for footpaths and red dashes for bridleways. On the OS 1:25 000 scale, the dots and dashes are green. (Red dots and dashes on the 1:25 000 Outdoor Leisure Maps indicate permitted footpaths and bridleways respectively). All of the walks in this guide cover routes which follow the public right of way.

4   THE COUNTRY CODE

The Country Code has been designed not as a set of hard and fast rules, although they do have the backing of the law, but as a statement of common sense. The code is a gentle reminder of how to behave in the countryside. Walkers should walk with the intention of leaving the place exactly as it was before they arrived. There is an old saying that a good walker 'leaves only footprints and takes only photographs', which really sums up the code perfectly.

Never walk more than two abreast on a footpath as you will erode more ground causing an unnatural widening of paths. Also try to avoid the spread of trodden ground around a boggy area. Mud soon cleans off boots but plant life is slow to grow back once it has been worn away.

Have respect for everything in the countryside, be it those beautiful flowers found along the way or a farmer's gate which is difficult to close. Stone walls were built at a time when labour costs were a fraction of those today and the special skills required to build or repair them have almost disappeared. Never climb over or on to stone walls: always use stiles and gates.

Dogs which chase sheep can cause them to lose their lambs and a farmer is within his rights if he shoots a dog which he believes is worrying his stock.

The moors and woodlands are often tinder dry in summer, so take care not to start a fire. A fire caused by something as simple as a discarded cigarette can burn for weeks, once it gets deep down into the underlying peat.

When walking across fields or enclosed land, make sure that you read the map carefully and avoid trespassing. As a rule, the line of a footpath or right of way, even when it is not clearly defined on the ground, can usually be followed by lining up stiles or gates.

5   MAP READING

Some people find map reading so easy that they can open a map and immediately relate it to the area of countryside in which they are standing. To others a map is as unintelligible as ancient Greek! A map is an accurate but flat picture of the three dimensional features of the countryside. Features such as roads, streams, woodlands and buildings are relatively easy to identify, either from their shape or position. Heights, on the other hand, can be difficult to interpret from the single dimension of a map. The one inch (1:63 360) maps indicate every 50 foot contour line, while the metricated 1:25 000 and 1:50 000 maps give the contours at 10 metre intervals. Summits and spot heights are also shown.

The best way to estimate the angle of a slope, as shown on any map, is to remember that if the contour lines come close together then the slope is steep – the closer the steeper.

Learn the symbols for features shown on the map and, when starting out on a walk, line up the map with one or more feature, which is recognisable both from the map and on the ground. In this way the map will be correctly positioned relative to the terrain. It should only be necessary to look from the map towards the footpath or objective of your walk and then make for it! This process is also useful for determining your position at any time during the walk.

Let's take the skill of map reading one stage further. Sometimes there are no easily recognisable features nearby. There may be the odd clump of trees and a building or two but none of them can be exactly related to the map. This is a frequent occurrence but there is a simple answer to the problem and this is where the use of a compass comes in. Simply place the map on the ground, or other flat surface, with the compass held gently above the map. Turn the map until the edge is parallel to the line of the compass needle, which should point to the top of the map. Lay the compass on the map and adjust the position of both, making sure that the compass needle still points to the top of the map and is parallel to the edge. By this method, the map is orientated in a north-south alignment. To find your position on the map, look out for prominent features and draw imaginary lines from them down on to the map. Your position is where these lines cross. This method of map reading takes a little practice before you can become proficient but it is worth the effort.

It is all too easy for members of a walking group to leave map reading to the skilled member or members of the party. No one is perfect and even the best map reader can make mistakes. Other members of the group should take the trouble to follow the route on the map, so that any errors are spotted before they cause problems.

Once you become proficient at map reading, you will learn to estimate the length of time required for a walk. Generally, you should estimate an extra five minutes for every 100 ft (30.5m) you walk uphill.

6   THE PEAK DISTRICT NATIONAL PARK

In many other countries, National Parks are wilderness areas, where few people live unless they are connected with running the park. Countries such as the United States of America have even gone to the length of moving residents off land designated as National Park. In England and Wales, National Parks are areas of outstanding beauty where people still live and work. One of the major functions of a National Park is to preserve the landscape and the livelihoods of the people living within its boundaries. This is achieved by careful planning control. The *National Parks and Access to the Countryside Act* of 1949 led to the formation of the nine National Parks in England and Wales. The Peak National Park was designated as such in 1951.

The word National in the title sometimes leads to misunderstanding. National Parks are not nationalised or in any way owned by the government. Most of the land within the park is privately owned by the people who live and work there – be they farmers, private landowners or quarry owners. Certain areas of scenic beauty and ancient buildings around the Peak District are owned by The National Trust but these were left as gifts by far-sighted owners as a means of ensuring their preservation.

The Peak National Park extends over 542 square miles (1404 sq.km). Divided into two uniquely different zones, with wild gritstone moors to the north and gentler limestone uplands and dales to the south, it is surrounded by millions of people living in the industrial areas of England. With the advent of motorways the Peak is accessible to the bulk of the population in under two hours. The Peak District was the first National Park and is the most visited.

Administration of the park is controlled by a committee composed, on a proportional basis, of representatives of the surrounding County and Metropolitan Councils and two District Councils as well as members appointed by the Secretary of State for the Environment.

One of the statutory functions of a Park Authority is the appointment of full-time and voluntary Park Rangers. These are people with particular knowlege of some aspects of the local environment who are available to give help and advice to visitors. Other functions of the Ranger Service include giving assistance to local farmers in such matters as rebuilding damaged walls to prevent stock from straying and leading guided walks from one of the Information Centres. Permanent Information Centres are based at Edale, Castleton and Bakewell.

Probably the most important responsibility of the Peak National Park, from the point of view of the walker, is the negotiation of access agreements across open moorland. During the late 1920s and early 1930s, rambling grew in popularity as workers from the industrial towns looked for a means of escaping their crowded existence. The obvious place for this escape was to the high moors which were jealously guarded by their owners, who used them for grouse shooting. Pressures caused by the demand for easy and free access often led to conflicts of interest.

Several ramblers, mainly the alleged ring leaders, were arrested and received sentences ranging from two to six months but they had made their point. One of the first tasks the Peak National Park set itself after its formation in 1951 was to negotiate access agreements. These were not always straightforward but, by careful and diplomatic negotiation, agreements have been reached with farmers and landowners giving free access to most of the high moors of the Dark Peak. In all, a total of 76 square miles (197km^2) of moorland, including Kinder Scout, are open to unrestricted walking and rock climbing apart from a few days in summer when sections of the moors are closed for grouse shooting. Notices are published locally showing the dates when the moors are closed and there are also signposts giving dates at access points to the moors.

Losehill Hall National Park Study Centre is a converted Victorian mansion which is set in spaciously wooded grounds to the south of Lose Hill. Residential and day courses are held on a wide variety of topics ranging from environmental studies, archaeology and the National Park and the pressures it faces, to hill walking, cycling, caving and more specialised subjects.

7   WHAT IS THE PEAK DISTRICT?

The title Peak District is something of a misnomer. For a start there are only two or three hills in the district which can claim to represent the true conical shape of a peak. The name Peak, in fact, refers to a tribe who lived in the area in ancient times. In the year 924, a cleric writing about the hills and dales of what is now North Derbyshire, referred to the inhabitants as living in Peaclond and the name seems to have stuck. 'Peac' comes from the old English for knoll or hill: there is a hilly or mountainous meaning to the title, but certainly not peaks in the strictest sense. Another Old English reference occurs in the use of 'low' which comes from 'hlaw' meaning a mound or a hill. No wonder visitors are often confused – peaks where there are none and high points called lows!

There are really two Peak Districts – Dark and White. Two areas so completely different that, when standing on the breezy limestone plateau of the White Peak, it is hard to imagine that the untamed wilderness of Bleaklow and Kinder Scout are not far way.

Broadly speaking, the Peak District can be sub-divided into six distinct areas:

a   The most northerly is the wildest and covers the moors above Saddleworth and the Longdendale Valley with the huge spread of Bleaklow filling the space between Longdendale and the Snake Pass.

b   Kinder Scout is a vast boggy plateau bordered to its south by Edale and the graceful sweep of the Mam Tor/Rushup Edge Ridge.

c   To the east, rising above the Derwent valley, there is a long escarpment which is clearly defined by a series of gritstone edges backed by heather moorland.

d   In the west, gritstone crags range from The Roaches above Leek to Windgather Rocks and Castle Naze on the northern limits. High open moors offer miles of lesser known walking. Tranquil wooded valleys cutting the western moors are excellent places to walk on hot summer days.

e   Limestone makes its most northerly appearance in dramatic cliffs and knolls above Castleton, a place of caves and ancient lead mines. South of Castleton are some of the highest villages in the White Peak. They can expect to be cut of by deep snow for several days during most winters.

f   The limestone plateau to the southwest of the A6 is incised by deep valleys and is judged by many to be the prettiest part of the Peak. It is certainly a zone of contrasts where the lush pastures of the rolling uplands have been grazed by cattle since time immemorial. Rivers run pure and clear and they are full of lively trout.

People came early to the Peak. Settling first on the treeless limestone plateau, they left mysterious mounds and stone circles. The circle at Arbor Low between Hartington and Youlgreave was probably the most important. Certainly its surrounding earthworks indicate its significance. Arbor Low is unique as the stones lie flat, unlike the more normal uprights associated with other circles. Early man hunted in the Dark Peak, following the seasonal migrations of game across moorland then covered by scrubby birch and mountain ash. Oak trees filled most of the valleys and dales and made them impregnable until later dwellers cut the trees down for fuel and building material. During later and less settled areas, massive earthworks were constructed at different times on top of Mam Tor and at Carl Wark.

Lead brought the Romans into the Peak. The metal, which was mined long before their arrival, attracted them to the area and they established their main cente at *Lutadarum*. Lead ingots embossed with this name have been found and an archaeological survey indicates that *Lutadarum* was probably near Wirksworth. Further north, a fort was built at *Navio* below the village of Hope, to control the hostile natives.

Following the Norman Conquest, the northern part of the Peak was designated a royal game forest or *frith* (hence Chapel-en-le Frith).

William Peveril, illegitimate son of the Conquerer, had a castle built on an easily defendable crag above Castleton. The castle controlled the King's lead mining interests as well as providing a base for hunting expeditions.

During the Middle Ages, most of the lands were owned by various monasteries. They continued to exploit the resources of lead, which were then very much in demand both as a roofing material and for constructing pipes to supply water into a growing number of monastic establishments. The monks opened large tracts of arable grazing and produced wool to clothe an expanding population. Farms which today have the word Grange as part of their name, were owned by rich monastries until their dissolution by Henry VIII.

Great houses have been built in the Peak. Some are well known, like Chatsworth with its parkland, which was landscaped by Capability Brown, or Haddon Hall – a uniquely preserved medieval country house. There are also many lesser-known stately homes throughout the district which are just as interesting. Most are in private hands, like Tissington Hall which has been owned by the same family for generations. Hartington Hall, a fine example of a Jacobean yeoman's house is now a youth hostel as is Ilam Hall which is an early Victorian manion preserved by the National Trust.

Customs and festivals abound in the Peak: a unique and charming custom is 'well dressing'. Pictures, usually of a biblical theme, are made from colourful petals, mosses and twigs stuck onto wet clay. The origins of this delightful custom, which offers thanks for the plentiful supply of water on the dry limestone plateau, are lost in the mists of time. A dozen or so villages dress their wells each year and details of the dates are included in the Peak Park's calendar of events. Local Shrovetide customs include the pancake race in Winster and a football match in Ashbourne where almost anything goes. A more tranquil custom is the Castleton Garland Procession. Although linked to ancient fertility rites, it always takes place on 29 May (Oak Apple Day) in commemoration of the restoration to the throne of Charles II. Also, the annual Love Feast is held on the first Sunday in July in a barn in Alport Dale, high above Snake Road. This is a link with times when dissenting worshippers, who disagreed with the 'Act of Uniformity' tying them to the Church of England, had to find seclusion away from the attentions of the troops of the reinstated King Charles II. Forest Chapel, near Wildboarclough, has a rush bearing ceremony on the Sunday nearest to 12 August each year.

Visitors to the Peak can buy jewellery made from Blue John, a semi precious stone found only beneath Treak Cliff, near Castleton. Another Peak novelty is the Bakewell Pudding (never call it a tart!) This delicacy was first made accidently by a 19th-century cook working in the Rutland Arms Hotel. Fine Stilton cheese is made at the dairy in Hartington from the milk of Peakland cows.

Famous writers have penned the virtues of the Peak but none has better links than Izaak Walton, who fished the Dove with Charles Cotton.

Industry has always made its mark. Pack horse, or 'jaggers' tracks can still be followed on foot over the northern moors. Saltways cross the southern dales. Water-powered mills in the early part of the Industrial Revolution brought textile production to the dales. Florspar, a nuisance to the early lead miners, is now extracted by open cast mining and used as a flux in steel making and as the basis for a number of chemicals.

Today, without any doubt, it is quarrying which makes the greatest industrial impact on the face of the Peak District. Limestone, suitable either as road aggregates or for cement making, is only found in scenically attractive areas and, as a result, the quarries can make an ugly scar on the landscape unless they are carefully monitored.

8 GEOLOGY

The rocks which made the foundations of the Peak District were laid down millions of years ago in a warm sea. Miriads of sea creatures living on the slimy bottom built up the great depth of limestone. Tropical lagoons were fringed by coral reefs which, through time, have become the rounded hills of Thorpe Cloud, Parkhouse and Chrome Hills in Dove Dale. Minor volcanic activity took place during this time. The best examples of this can be found in the small outcrops of basalt near Castleton and in the dolerite quarry which is part of the Tideswell Dale Nature Trail. Lead found its way in gaseous form, through minute cracks in the underlying rocks, laying down the basis of what became a major industry thousands of centuries later. Copper was also deposited in this way, occurring beneath Ecton Hill in the Manifold valley.

A mighty river delta flooded into the tropical sea, depositing mud and sand which consolidated to make the gritstones of the Dark Peak and the shales of Mam Tor.

Gradually, the layers of limestone and gritstone bulged from pressures deep within the earth and the middle and edges split. Ice action later honed the land into the beginning of the Peak District's rocky pattern. At the end of the Ice Age, huge volumes of melt water continued this shaping. The water carved caverns within the limestone of Castleton and Matlock as well as the pot holes of Eldon and it also created the beautiful dales. The land tilted as it buckled to give west facing gristone outcrops on both sides of the Peak.

9   WILDLIFE IN THE PEAK

Grouse spend their hardy lives on the high moors of the Dark Peak feeding on the tender shoots of young heather. Their tough existence is rudely shattered for four months of every year beginning on the Glorious Twelfth of August. Not so common, and regrettably often shot by mistake, are their cousins the black grouse. Birds of prey have their chosen areas and many migrants, some quite rare, visit quieter sanctuaries on the moors from time to time. Mountain hares are common despite an inability to quickly shed their winter camouflage once the snows have gone. Foxes live a frugal life, mainly dependent upon voles and other small creatures. Plant life on the acid moors has to be tough to combat the extreme weather conditions. Heathers, coarse grass and berry plants such as bilberry, cloudberry and crowberry manage to survive in this harsh environment.

The limestone plateau is much more gentle. It is mainly given over to grazing and masses of colourful flowers still fill the hayfields and road verges. Scabious, meadow cranesbill and other plants, which were once scarce, have made a recent comeback in fields where far-sighted farmers have moved back to natural and cheaper methods of fertilising the land. Plant, and to a certain extent animal life, in the Dales depends on the underlying strata. The Upper Derwent and its tributaries flow mostly through shale and gritstone. Forests planted around the Derwent Reservoirs are a major feature and offer homes to woodland birds and a few deer as well as smaller carnivorous animals. In the limestone dales, trees were once cut down for fuel but they are plentiful today and, in some instances, are crowding other plant life. In Dove Dale, a courageous scheme has removed much of the invasive woodland to recreate more open vistas. Plant life on the craggy scree-covered hillsides is mostly dwarf and with an almost alpine quality.

But the dales are best known for their trout streams. Not only do game fish breed in their clear waters but crayfish, a crustacean which needs pure water, is found beneath the rocks of most of the rivers in the dales.

10   LONG DISTANCE WALKS IN THE PEAK

Cal-Derwent Walk: a high level moorland route linking the Calder and Derwent valleys.

Derbyshire Gritstone Way: follows gritstone edges above the River Derwent from Edale to Derby.

Gritstone Trail: waymarked route along the western edge of the Peak District from Lyme Park to Mow Cop near Rudyard Lake where it links with the Staffordshire Way.

Limestone Way: a route waymarked with the Derby Ram symbol from Matlock to Castleton across the limestone uplands.

The Pennine Way: Britain's first long distance footpath starts at Edale and follows a high level route along the Pennines to finish at Kirk Yetholm in Scotland.

The White Peak Way: a circular walk around the southern half of the Peak National Park. Easily divides into seven stages based on Bakewell, Elton, Ilam Hall, Hartington, Ravenstor, Castleton and Hathersage youth hostels.

Trails based on disused railways

High Peak Trail: follows the High Peak Railway (including Cromford Incline) from Cromford Wharf to Sparklow. Cycle hire scheme.

Manifold Valley Trail: Macadam surfaced track of the Manifold Valley Light Railway from Hulme End to Waterhouses. Suitable for wheel chairs but please note that sections are used by motorised traffic. Cycle hire scheme.

Monsal Trail: starts at Bakewell station and follows the Midland Line to Miller's Dale. Diverges to avoid tunnels. Spectacular scenic views of Monsal Dale. Cycle hire scheme.

Sett Valley Trail: Hayfield to New Mills cycle trackway with linking footpaths.

Tissington Trail: uses part of the Ashbourne to Buxton line to link with the High Peak Trail at Parsley Hay. Cycle hire scheme.

11 USEFUL ADDRESSES

Peak District National Park
Aldern House
Baslow Road
Bakewell DE4 1AE
Derbyshire
Tel: (01629) 816200

Peak National Park Study Centre
Losehill Hall
Castleton S30 2WB
Derbyshire
Tel: (01433) 620373

Bakewell Information Centre
Old Market Hall
Bakewell
Tel: (01629) 813227

Buxton Information Centre
The Crescent
Buxton
Tel: (01298) 25106

Castleton Information Centre
Castles Street
Castleton
Tel: (01433) 620679

Edale Information Centre
Field Head
Edale
Tel: (01433) 670207

Ilam Country Park Information Centre
Ilam
Nr. Ashbourne
Tel: (01335) 350245

Matlock Bath Information Centre
The Pavillion
Matlock Bath
Tel: (01629) 55082

Temporary information centres are open at weekends and bank holidays throughout the summer months at:

Hartington Railway Station (Tissington Trail)

Torside (Longendale Valley)

Local and regional tourist offices can also be found at Ashbourne, Chesterfield, Leek, Macclesfield and Sheffield.

Walk 1
LYME PARK AND SPONDS HILL
5 miles (8km) Easy/Moderate; one 478ft (146m) climb

0   ½ mile

0   1 km

Lyme Hall was the home of the Legh family for many generations but death duties and running costs forced them to relinquish this fine Palladian house and its deer park.

This is a popular walk which offers unrivalled views of the house and its formal grounds and then climbs to open breezy moorland heights.

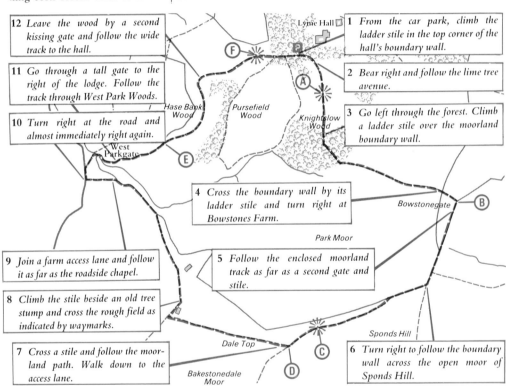

12 Leave the wood by a second kissing gate and follow the wide track to the hall.

11 Go through a tall gate to the right of the lodge. Follow the track through West Park Woods.

10 Turn right at the road and almost immediately right again.

9 Join a farm access lane and follow it as far as the roadside chapel.

8 Climb the stile beside an old tree stump and cross the rough field as indicated by waymarks.

7 Cross a stile and follow the moorland path. Walk down to the access lane.

1 From the car park, climb the ladder stile in the top corner of the hall's boundary wall.

2 Bear right and follow the lime tree avenue.

3 Go left through the forest. Climb a ladder stile over the moorland boundary wall.

4 Cross the boundary wall by its ladder stile and turn right at Bowstones Farm.

5 Follow the enclosed moorland track as far as a second gate and stile.

6 Turn right to follow the boundary wall across the open moor of Sponds Hill.

Lyme Hall

Hase Bank Wood

Pursefield Wood

Knightslow Wood

West Parkgate

Bowstonegate

Park Moor

Sponds Hill

Dale Top

Bakestonedale Moor

A View of Lyme Hall across its ornamental lake.

B Bowstones. These are the two stone pillars enclosed by a low metal fence near the farm entrance. The name suggests that they might have been used in the making of bows but they probably predate these weapons.

C Viewpoint. Lyme Hall can be seen beyond its surrounding pine woods.

D The hollows on Dale Top were once shallow coal pits.

E In May and June rhododendrons make a contrasting splash of pink and red against the dark green of the pines.

F Viewpoint. The Palladian frontage of Lyme Hall is seen to its best advantage here. The Dutch garden is worth closer examination, especially in the late spring when the tulips are in full bloom.

Walk 2
MACCLESFIELD FOREST AND SHUTLINGSLOE
7 miles (11.3km) Strenuous; one 759ft (231m) climb

0 _____ 1 mile
0 _____ 1 km

Shutlingsloe is not the highest point of normally flat Cheshire but it certainly has the best shape of any hill on this the western boundary of the Peak District. We cross its rocky summit on this walk through the Cheshire Uplands.

10 Turn right at the pub, then right along the minor road, following it all the way back to Trentabank Reservoir. Keep right at all road junctions.

1 From the lay-by car park, climb the short flight of steps and then cross a stile. Walk uphill along the broad path through mature pine forest.

Macclesfield Forest
Chapel
Bottom-of-
the-Oven

Macclesfield
Forest
Trentabank
Reservoir

9 Bear right across rough moorland pasture and then left, downhill on a sunken track, aiming directly towards the Hanging Gate Inn.

2 Cross the stile in the upper forest boundary. Follow the signposted path out on to the open moor.

8 Keep below and left of both Oak-enclough House and Farm. Cross the stream and climb to the access drive. Cross this and turn left up-hill along an enclosed footpath.

High Moor
Oakenclough

Shutlingsloe Farm

3 Climb the stile and bear right over a stretch of boggy moor. Aim for the prominent summit of Shutl-ingsloe.

Crag
Hall

7 Cross a stile on the right by the side of Greenway Bridge. Follow waymarks upstream towards Oakenclough. Keep left at the junction with a lesser stream and then right of a small ruined barn.

Piggford Moor
Greenway
Bridge
Wildboarclough

6 Climb the stile and join the farm lane near a sharp bend. Turn left and follow the lane as far as the road, then turn right.

5 Climb the flight of steps in the roadside wall at the corner of the pub car park. Follow the grassy path above a clump of thorn bushes. Cross a series of pathless fields as indicated by waymarks and stiles.

4 Follow yellow arrows, steeply downhill through the summit rocks and across the lower moor. Cross the boundary wall by its stile and, still following waymarks, keep well to the right of the farm buildings. Turn right on the access drive and join the valley road conveniently close to the Crag Inn.

A Trentabank Reservoir Nature Reserve. A plaque shows the commonest visiting and resident waterfowl on this attractive reservoir within Macclesfield Forest.

B Shutlingsloe, 1659ft (506m). A commemorative plaque in the summit rocks gives the names of the prominent features seen from this vantage point. The valley, which the route next follows, is Wildboarclough and the ornamental lake opposite is within the grounds of Crag Hall, part of the estate of Lord Derby.

C Viewpoint. Shutlingsloe is opposite, above Piggford Moor.

D Viewpoint. Tegg's Nose Country Park includes the over-grown quarries on the skyline. Below, the mature pines of Mac-clesfield Forest fill the valley and the scene is completed by Lang-ley's twin reservoirs.

13

Walk 3
THE ROACHES
7 miles (11.3km) Moderate/Strenuous; one 608ft (185m) climb

The Roaches provide some of the finest and longest gritstone climbs in the Peak District. This is where many of the famous local climbers such as Joe Brown and the late Don Whillans first developed their skills. Routes of every standard can be found on these crags and climbers will be seen almost every day of the year attempting what might seem impossibly acrobatic moves.

French monks established their Dieulacresse Abbey close by; below what is now Tittesworth Reservoir. They, with what in hindsight sounds like a lack of imagination, gave the crags the name 'Rocher' which is French for 'rock'. The name changed to Roaches at a later date but lingers in the old form at Roche Grange.

Today the moors and the Roaches themselves are owned by the Peak Park Planning Board. In buying the Roaches Estate, the Board have opened up access to the rocks for climbers and also established a number of concessionary footpaths over the moors, several of which are used to advantage on this walk.

About half way along the walk, the route passes through Lud Church, a roofless fern bedecked cave caused by a landslip in the gritstone strata. This strange gorge is linked with legends and it can be a spooky place on the sunniest of days.

Do not be alarmed if you see wallabies on this walk. It will have nothing to do with any pre-walk visit to the nearby Rock Inn! There really are wallabies on the moors around the Roaches. These marsupials are the descendants of animals released during World War II from a private zoo established by Lt. Col. Brocklehurst who had been a game warden in the Sudan. At one time there was even a yak wandering about on the moors, much to the consternation of unsuspecting walkers and climbers!

A small number of wallabies have managed to survive despite the harsh winters. Please respect these shy creatures and do not try to find them. Keep dogs under control at all times and you may be rewarded by an unexpected glimpse of these strange creatures.

A Rockhall Cottage. As this building is inhabited, please do not attempt to climb the perimeter wall.

B Viewpoint. The dramatic peak of Hen Cloud is to the southeast. Beyond, the North Staffordshire Plain stretches into the distance.

C Doxey Pool. This little pool does not appear to have either an inlet or outlet.

D Viewpoint. Shutlingsloe, Cheshire's 'Matterhorn', rises above the Dane Valley and the hills of North Wales can often be seen in hazy outline across the Cheshire Plain. Approximately due west, The Cloud can be seen.

E Lud's Church. It is said that the cave was a refuge for Walter de Ludank, a follower of Wycliffe who held dissenting services here in the 14th century. A more ancient legend connects it with the Green Chapel of the medieval poem 'Sir Gawain and the Green Knight'. If this is correct, then it was on this spot that King Arthur's champion met and fought the green knight.

F Viewpoint. Castle Cliff Rocks make an ideal picnic spot above the Upper Dane.

G Viewpoint. The nearby valley is the Dane.

H At one time there were many small farms in this area. Their owners eked out a bare living by mining coal in shallow pits on the moors. Many of the small holdings still exist, with the present day owners working in nearby towns and farming in their spare time.

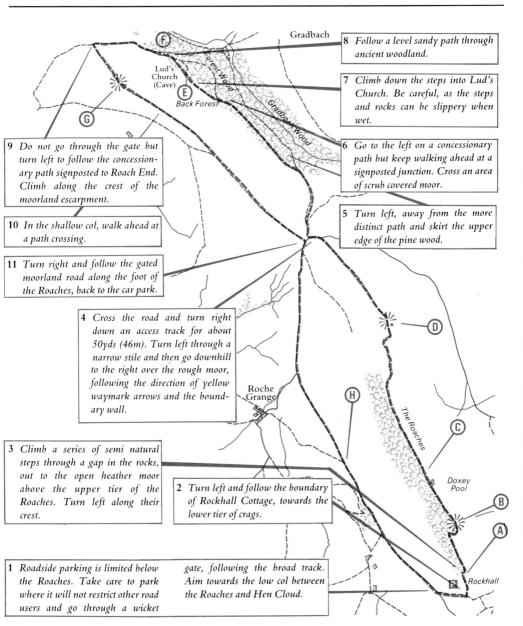

Gradbach

Lud's
Church
(Cave) Ⓔ

Ⓕ

Forest Wood

Back Forest

Gradbach Wood

Ⓖ

8 Follow a level sandy path through ancient woodland.

7 Climb down the steps into Lud's Church. Be careful, as the steps and rocks can be slippery when wet.

9 Do not go through the gate but turn left to follow the concessionary path signposted to Roach End. Climb along the crest of the moorland escarpment.

6 Go to the left on a concessionary path but keep walking ahead at a signposted junction. Cross an area of scrub covered moor.

10 In the shallow col, walk ahead at a path crossing.

5 Turn left, away from the more distinct path and skirt the upper edge of the pine wood.

11 Turn right and follow the gated moorland road along the foot of the Roaches, back to the car park.

4 Cross the road and turn right down an access track for about 50yds (46m). Turn left through a narrow stile and then go downhill to the right over the rough moor, following the direction of yellow waymark arrows and the boundary wall.

Roche
Grange

Ⓗ

Ⓓ

The Roaches

Ⓒ

3 Climb a series of semi natural steps through a gap in the rocks, out to the open heather moor above the upper tier of the Roaches. Turn left along their crest.

2 Turn left and follow the boundary of Rockhall Cottage, towards the lower tier of crags.

Doxey
Pool

Ⓑ

Ⓐ

1 Roadside parking is limited below the Roaches. Take care to park where it will not restrict other road users and go through a wicket gate, following the broad track. Aim towards the low col between the Roaches and Hen Cloud.

Rockhall

15

Walk 4
SOLOMON'S TEMPLE
4½ miles (7.2km) Easy; uphill sections

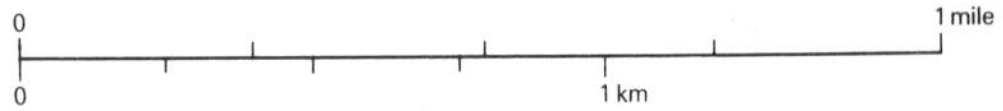

0
1 mile
0
1 km

Buxton has retained many of the attractions from its heyday as a spa town when visitors combined 'taking the waters' with an inland holiday. Re-opened after being abandoned for years, Pooles Cavern and its Visitor Centre give an interesting insight into the archaeological past.

The walk skirts Grin Low Woods and then climbs out on to the stark limestone moors before moving to Solomon's Temple with its vantage point above the town.

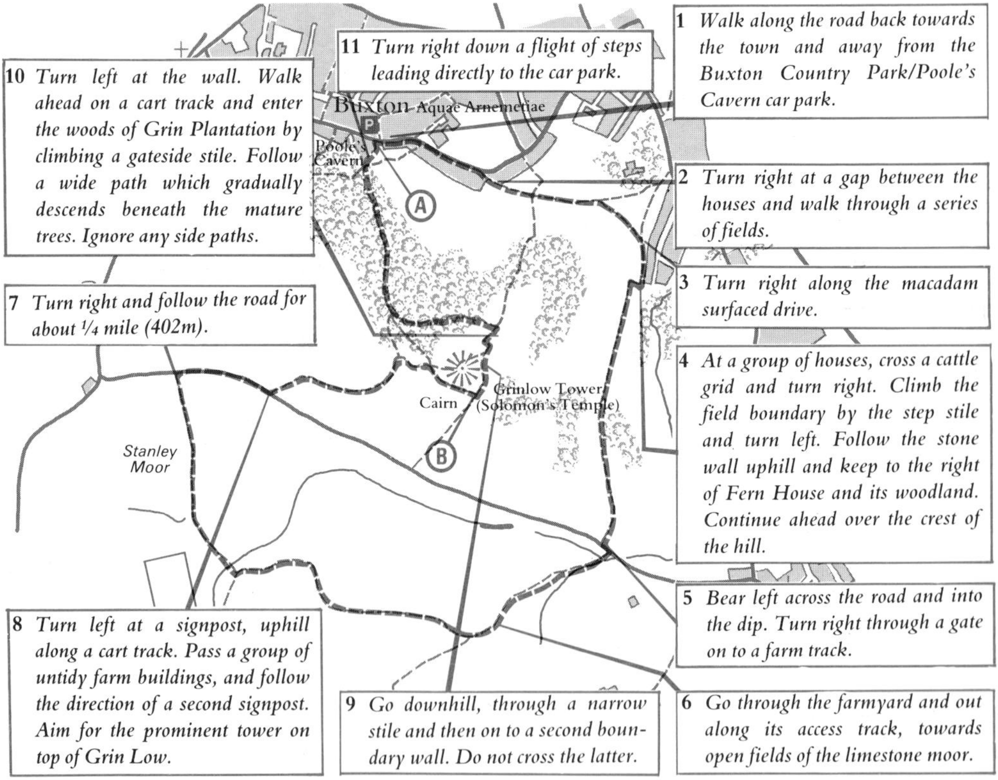

Buxton Aquae Arnemetiae
P
Poole's Cavern
A
B
Cairn
Grinlow Tower (Solomon's Temple)
Stanley Moor

1 *Walk along the road back towards the town and away from the Buxton Country Park/Poole's Cavern car park.*

2 *Turn right at a gap between the houses and walk through a series of fields.*

3 *Turn right along the macadam surfaced drive.*

4 *At a group of houses, cross a cattle grid and turn right. Climb the field boundary by the step stile and turn left. Follow the stone wall uphill and keep to the right of Fern House and its woodland. Continue ahead over the crest of the hill.*

5 *Bear left across the road and into the dip. Turn right through a gate on to a farm track.*

6 *Go through the farmyard and out along its access track, towards open fields of the limestone moor.*

7 *Turn right and follow the road for about ¼ mile (402m).*

8 *Turn left at a signpost, uphill along a cart track. Pass a group of untidy farm buildings, and follow the direction of a second signpost. Aim for the prominent tower on top of Grin Low.*

9 *Go downhill, through a narrow stile and then on to a second boundary wall. Do not cross the latter.*

10 *Turn left at the wall. Walk ahead on a cart track and enter the woods of Grin Plantation by climbing a gateside stile. Follow a wide path which gradually descends beneath the mature trees. Ignore any side paths.*

11 *Turn right down a flight of steps leading directly to the car park.*

A Poole's Cavern. Classed as the 'First wonder of the Peak' by Charles Cotton in 1680, the natural cave was once the home of Stone Age Man. Open from Easter to early November, its history is explained in the adjacent Visitor Centre. Derbyshire's River Wye starts from this cave.

B Do not worry if you hear explosions coming from the strange cluster of buildings opposite. This is the Explosion and Fire Laboratory of the Health and Safety Executive where hazardous mixtures are tested under controlled conditions.

C Solomon's Temple. The tower was built in 1895 for a local worthy called Solomon Mycock, as a Victorian kind of job creation scheme. It sits on top of a prehistoric mound and at 1300ft (396m) it makes an excellent vantage point above Buxton and the surrounding moors.

Walk 5
COMBS
4 miles (6.4km) Moderate; muddy sections

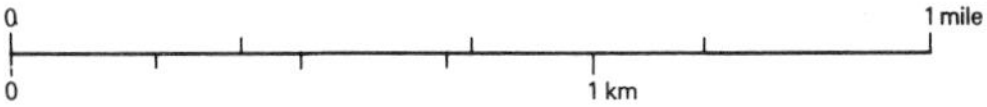

```
0                                          1 mile
|----+----+----+----+----+----|
0                        1 km
```

The walk starts and finishes at the | pleasant village of Combs, which | moorland of Combs Moss, a little
Beehive Inn, a focal point of the | nestles snugly beneath the wild | known outlier of the Dark Peak.

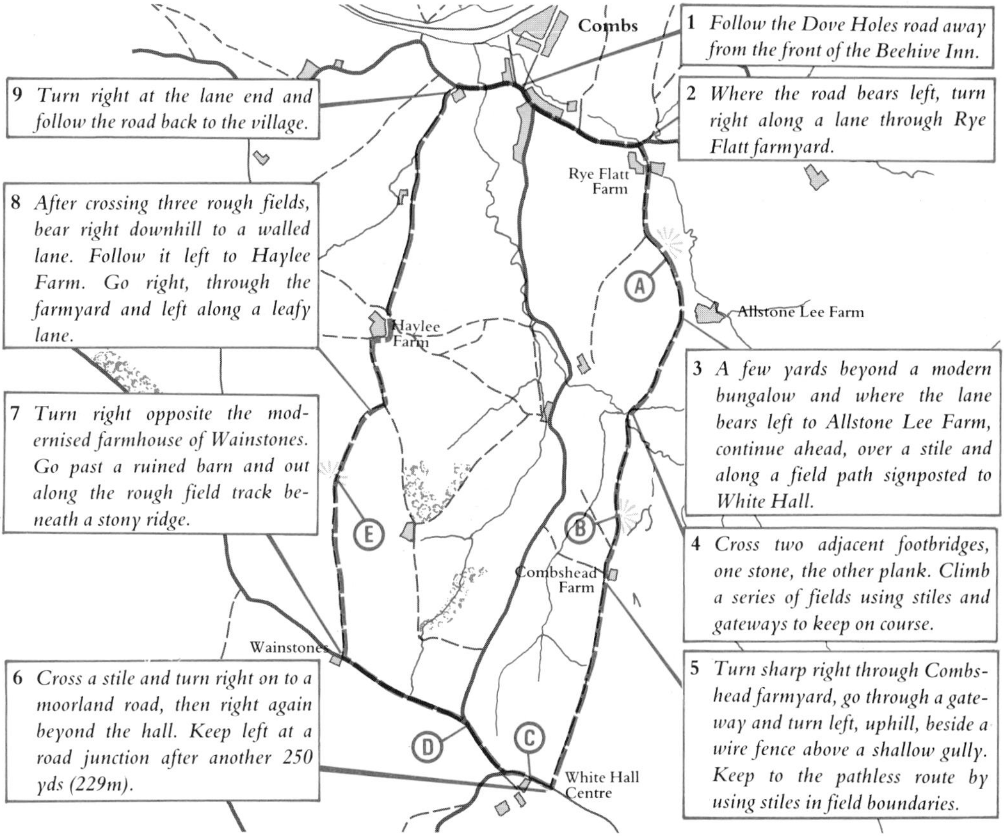

1 *Follow the Dove Holes road away from the front of the Beehive Inn.*

2 *Where the road bears left, turn right along a lane through Rye Flatt farmyard.*

9 *Turn right at the lane end and follow the road back to the village.*

8 *After crossing three rough fields, bear right downhill to a walled lane. Follow it left to Haylee Farm. Go right, through the farmyard and left along a leafy lane.*

3 *A few yards beyond a modern bungalow and where the lane bears left to Allstone Lee Farm, continue ahead, over a stile and along a field path signposted to White Hall.*

7 *Turn right opposite the modernised farmhouse of Wainstones. Go past a ruined barn and out along the rough field track beneath a stony ridge.*

4 *Cross two adjacent footbridges, one stone, the other plank. Climb a series of fields using stiles and gateways to keep on course.*

5 *Turn sharp right through Combshead farmyard, go through a gateway and turn left, uphill, beside a wire fence above a shallow gully. Keep to the pathless route by using stiles in field boundaries.*

6 *Cross a stile and turn right on to a moorland road, then right again beyond the hall. Keep left at a road junction after another 250 yds (229m).*

Map labels: Combs, Rye Flatt Farm, Allstone Lee Farm, Haylee Farm, Combshead Farm, Wainstones, White Hall Centre, A, B, C, D, E

A Viewpoint. The private grouse moor of Combs Moss is in front. To the left are the crags of Castle Naze, a favourite training ground for local rock climbers. Behind the rocks and out of sight, a solid earthen bank marks the limits of an Iron Age fort.

B Viewpoint. The slopes below

the building on the skyline to the left are covered by bracken which will not grow on the windy heights beyond the moorland edge. That region is given over to heather and bilberry.

C White Hall is an Outdoor Pursuits Centre run by Derbyshire County Council.

D The road follows the route between Roman Arnemetia (Buxton) and Mancunium (Manchester).

E Viewpoint. Combs village fits snugly in a wide hollow beneath its Moss. In the distance, to your half left, is Kinder Scout and its outliers.

17

Walk 6
RUSHUP EDGE
5½ miles (8.8km) Moderate; one 1029ft (314m) climb

The climb to reach the summit of Rushup Edge is amply rewarded with superb views. In the north the gritstone plateau of Kinder Scout rises menacingly above Edale but, to the south, the White Peak and its limestone based pasture is far gentler. The boundary between these geological contrasts is followed by the A625 road at the foot of Rushup Edge.

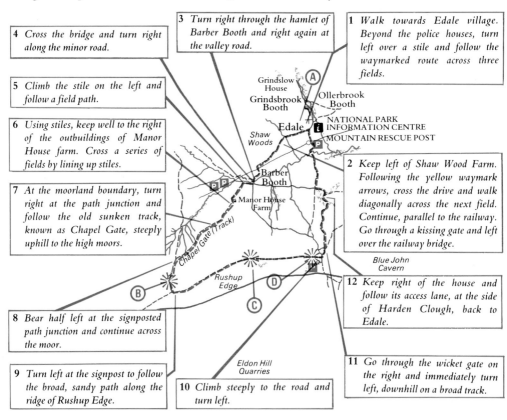

4 Cross the bridge and turn right along the minor road.

5 Climb the stile on the left and follow a field path.

6 Using stiles, keep well to the right of the outbuildings of Manor House farm. Cross a series of fields by lining up stiles.

7 At the moorland boundary, turn right at the path junction and follow the old sunken track, known as Chapel Gate, steeply uphill to the high moors.

8 Bear half left at the signposted path junction and continue across the moor.

9 Turn left at the signpost to follow the broad, sandy path along the ridge of Rushup Edge.

3 Turn right through the hamlet of Barber Booth and right again at the valley road.

Grindslow House
Grindsbrook Booth
Ollerbrook Booth
Edale
Shaw Woods
NATIONAL PARK INFORMATION CENTRE
MOUNTAIN RESCUE POST
Barber Booth
Manor House Farm
Chapel Gate (Track)
Rushup Edge
Eldon Hill Quarries

10 Climb steeply to the road and turn left.

1 Walk towards Edale village. Beyond the police houses, turn left over a stile and follow the waymarked route across three fields.

2 Keep left of Shaw Wood Farm. Following the yellow waymark arrows, cross the drive and walk diagonally across the next field. Continue, parallel to the railway. Go through a kissing gate and left over the railway bridge.

Blue John Cavern

12 Keep right of the house and follow its access lane, at the side of Harden Clough, back to Edale.

11 Go through the wicket gate on the right and immediately turn left, downhill on a broad track.

A Call in at the Fieldhead National Park Information Centre to get the local weather forecast.

B Viewpoint. To the southwest, Combs Moss rises above Chapel-en-le-Frith. Beyond, the limestone plateau of White Peak.

C Viewpoint. Lord's Seat Tumulus. To the north, rocky outcrops on Kinder Scout stand out from the stark moor. In contrast to the south, the panorama is totally limestone.

D Viewpoint. The ramparts of a prehistoric fort stand out sharply on Mam Tor.

E Shales lining Mam Nick are as those which cause the slipping of Mam Tor's south face.

Walk 7
BIRCHEN EDGE
4 miles (6.4km) Moderate

0   1 mile

0   1 km

Two monoliths, erected in memory of Nelson and Wellington, make excellent route markers for this walk. The route crosses stark gritstone edges on the skyline above Bar Brook, which offer magnificent views of the surrounding moors and parkland.

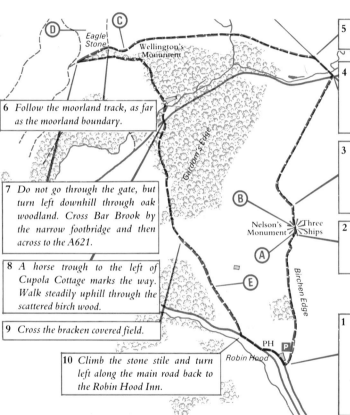

5 Go left through a gate on to a turf covered moorland track.

4 Climb a ladder stile and turn left on the road. Follow it with great care across the busy A621 Sheffield road. Walk uphill, opposite, for about 150 yards (137m).

6 Follow the moorland track, as far as the moorland boundary.

3 At the triangulation pillar, turn left downhill through the narrow gap in the crag. Turn right along a narrow moorland path following occasional wooden marker posts.

7 Do not go through the gate, but turn left downhill through oak woodland. Cross Bar Brook by the narrow footbridge and then across to the A621.

2 Take care on reaching the lower part of the crag and follow the path through a rocky gap. Turn left along the summit rocks.

8 A horse trough to the left of Cupola Cottage marks the way. Walk steadily uphill through the scattered birch wood.

9 Cross the bracken covered field.

1 Park near the Robin Hood Inn above the A619 Chesterfield road. Walk past the adjoining cottage and climb a ladder stile on the left. Follow the rocky, woodland path uphill, aiming for the crest of Birchen Edge.

10 Climb the stone stile and turn left along the main road back to the Robin Hood Inn.

A Nelson's Monument. Nearby are three boulders, each shaped like the bow of a man-of-war. They are fancifully named *Victory*, *Defiance* and *Soverin*; all ships at the Battle of Trafalgar.

B Viewpoint. Chatsworth House and its park fills the valley. To the left is the largest expanse of grouse moor in the Southern Pennines.

C Wellington Monument. The stone cross was erected in 1866. From here, there is a good view of Chatsworth House.

D The Eagle Stone is slightly off route but can be reached by a narrow sidepath. At one time, every young man from Baslow had to climb it before he could get married.

E A bracken covered mound, about halfway across the last field before the road, is the site of a prehistoric enclosure.

Walk 8
LADYBOWER
6½ miles (10.5km) Moderate; one 580ft (177m) climb

Here is a walk with contrasting views. Starting near the Ashopton viaduct, it leaves the reservoir by climbing steadily across the flank of Crook Hill along an ancient bridleway. This track carried people and goods between West Yorkshire and Cheshire, long before the Snake Road turnpike was built. The views from Crook Hill, especially those opposite, of the edges above the Derwent Valley, are most spectacular. Strange rock formations with fanciful names dot the eastern skyline and the eye is carried easily across the heights from scene to scene. Quiet forest glades lead down to the man-made lake of Ladybower where a quiet road is followed along its eastern shore, to the busy A57.

During summer weekends and bank holidays, the road from Fairholmes to the dale head is free of all but essential motor traffic. A mini bus service carries pedestrians to various points along the road and a cycle hire scheme helps visitors enjoy the tranquillity and beauty of this secluded valley.

A Crook Hill viewpoint. To the east, across the deep cleft of flooded Derwent Dale, the eastern skyline is marked by rocky outcrops, more in keeping with Dartmoor Tors. Most of the rocks are named but two, in particular, should be obvious from their shape, even at this distance: one is the 'Salt Cellar' and the other, the 'Coach & Horses' (marked 'Wheel Stones' on the OS map), is just like a 19th-century mail coach. Even though it is man-made and completely altered the appearance of the dale, Ladybower Reservoir makes an attractive contrast to the wild moors beyond.

Westward from Crook Hill and across the Woodlands Valley arm of the reservoir, are the heights of Win Hill and Kinder Scout.

B Viewpoint. Kinder Scout's northern edges dominate the Ashop Valley and over the northern shoulder of Win Hill, Mam Tor's undulating ridge marks the boundary between the Dark and White Peak. To the north, the underlying rocks were laid down by an ancient river delta millions of years ago. The river in its turn buried the even older limestone, deposited by countless sea creatures in a tropical sea.

C Viewpoint. From the farm look across Lockerbrook Plantation to Ladybower Reservoir and the Derwent Edges.

D Derwent Dam. When the reservoir is full, water cascades over the dam wall creating the largest waterfall in the Peak. The dam was used by members of the famous Dam Busters Squadron, when they were training for the wartime raids on the Möhne and Eder dams in the Ruhr. The same dam was used in the film portraying this courageous exploit.

E A plaque at the side of the Mill Brook tells the sad story of the lost village of Derwent. All that remains of this village is the re-erected war memorial on the roadside above the west shore of the reservoir. A graceful pack-horse bridge, which was sited near the village, now crosses the River Derwent at Slippery Stones almost at the head of the valley.

F There is another drowned village below this point. This was Ashopton, once reached by a steep tree-shrouded lane below the A57. It is hard to imagine, gazing out over millions of gallons of water, that the Derwent flowed past Ashopton on its way south through a deep rocky valley. All that tranquillity ended in 1943, when the sluices were shut and water drowned an idyllic valley with its farms and villages.

0   1 mile

0   1 km

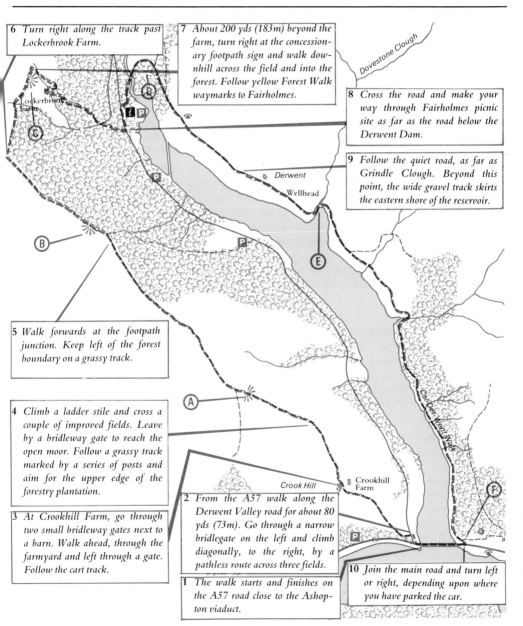

6 Turn right along the track past Lockerbrook Farm.

7 About 200 yds (183m) beyond the farm, turn right at the concessionary footpath sign and walk downhill across the field and into the forest. Follow yellow Forest Walk waymarks to Fairholmes.

8 Cross the road and make your way through Fairholmes picnic site as far as the road below the Derwent Dam.

9 Follow the quiet road, as far as Grindle Clough. Beyond this point, the wide gravel track skirts the eastern shore of the reservoir.

Dovestone Clough

Lockerbrook Farm

Derwent Wellhead

5 Walk forwards at the footpath junction. Keep left of the forest boundary on a grassy track.

4 Climb a ladder stile and cross a couple of improved fields. Leave by a bridleway gate to reach the open moor. Follow a grassy track marked by a series of posts and aim for the upper edge of the forestry plantation.

3 At Crookhill Farm, go through two small bridleway gates next to a barn. Walk ahead, through the farmyard and left through a gate. Follow the cart track.

Crook Hill Crookhill Farm

Cut Derwent Walk

2 From the A57 walk along the Derwent Valley road for about 80 yds (73m). Go through a narrow bridlegate on the left and climb diagonally, to the right, by a pathless route across three fields.

1 The walk starts and finishes on the A57 road close to the Ashopton viaduct.

10 Join the main road and turn left or right, depending upon where you have parked the car.

Walk 9
STANAGE EDGE
7 miles (11.3km) Easy/Moderate; 914ft (279m) climb

This is a walk steeped in romantic legend; Robin Hood's henchman, Little John, is reputed to be buried in Hathersage churchyard and the hero of Sherwood, had an almost inaccessible refuge in a cave on Stanage Edge. The long, dramatic escarpment, where rock climbers can be seen practicing their skillful moves, has been scaled by climbers since the 1890s and has over 500 routes of varying technical difficulty. High Lees Hall, lying in a sunny sheltered valley below the rocks, featured in Charlotte Brönte's romantic novel, *Jane Eyre*.

Millstones litter the slopes below Stanage Edge. Now used as symbolic boundary markers of the Peak National Park, they were once in great demand for making woodpulp.

A Hathersage church. Little John's grave is opposite the main door. St Michael's church was built in the 14th and 15th centuries but it lies within the circular mound of a religion pre-dating Christianity.

B Viewpoint looking uphill over the moors towards the rocky escarpment of Stanage Edge.

C Viewpoint. Hope Valley is to the far right with Eyam Moor to the left.

D Viewpoint looking down to the enigmatic rocks of Carl Wark Fort on the right of a plantation of mixed conifers. Burbage Rocks line the left upper rim of the valley.

E Viewpoint. This is one of the finest views in the Peak. The Derwent Edges reach towards the horizon and Rushup Edge, Win Hill, Kinder Scout and Bleaklow can be seen across the valley.

Southward, the view encompasses most of the uplands of the White Peak where clumps of trees on hilltops indicate ancient burial mounds. Millstones littering the foot of Stanage Edge were carved by stone-masons who then left them until required by the Scandinavian wood pulp industry. This trade died when longer-lasting steel rollers took over. The typical 'wheel' shape of these stones with flat outer rims, indicates their use as grindstones. Stones used for flour milling are usually bevelled.

F Robin Hood's Cave. This draughty opening in the rocks could well have been used by a local bandit in less settled times but it is unknown how this cave, and a well on nearby Longshaw Estate, came by the title.

G Viewpoint looking uphill towards the crags of Stanage Edge. The path at this point was once part of a pack horse way, an important link between Sheffield and Manchester.

H North Lees Hall. This three storied, semi-fortified manor house is something of a rarity so far south. It is similar in purpose to the pele towers of the Scottish Borders offering protection to owners in the upper storeys and their animals on the ground floor.

North Lees and its estate now cared for by the Peak National Park, for many generations was owned by the Eyre family, who were recorded amongst the bowmen at Agincourt.

Charlotte Brönte stayed at Hathersage Vicarage for three weeks in 1845 with her friend Ellen Massey and her novel *Jane Eyre* came as a result of that holiday. Many of the settings used in the story can be recognised as places around Hathersage. North Lees Hall is clearly identified as Thornfield Hall from which Jane fled.

10 Turn left through a break in the crags and continue downhill on a flagged path to the mountain rescue post and public toilets.

11 Turn right, on a wide track to North Lees Hall: go down its access drive.

12 Turn right and walk downhill along the metalled road.

9 Turn left at the 'Open Country' sign. Aim towards the prominent Cowper Stone. Climb the outcrop on its left and follow a level path along the top of Stanage Edge.

8 Go left along the road, past the junction with Ladybower road.

7 Cross the stile in the wire boundary fence and walk uphill on the moorland footpath

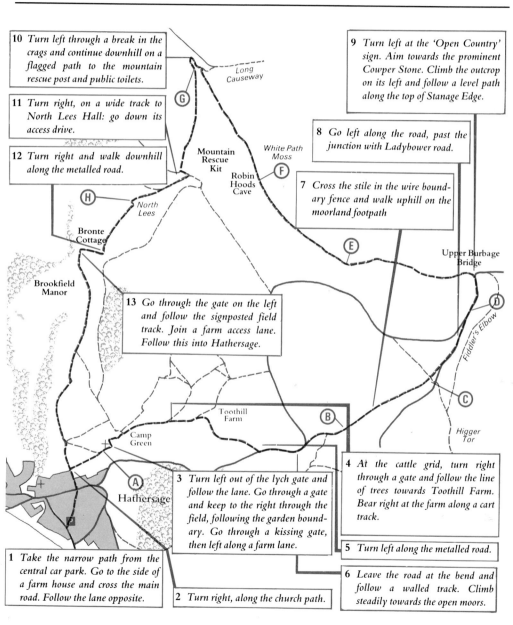

13 Go through the gate on the left and follow the signposted field track. Join a farm access lane. Follow this into Hathersage.

4 At the cattle grid, turn right through a gate and follow the line of trees towards Toothill Farm. Bear right at the farm along a cart track.

3 Turn left out of the lych gate and follow the lane. Go through a gate and keep to the right through the field, following the garden boundary. Go through a kissing gate, then left along a farm lane.

5 Turn left along the metalled road.

1 Take the narrow path from the central car park. Go to the side of a farm house and cross the main road. Follow the lane opposite.

2 Turn right, along the church path.

6 Leave the road at the bend and follow a walled track. Climb steadily towards the open moors.

Walk 10
MILLER'S DALE AND WORMHILL
5 miles (8km) Moderate

Airy upland pastures on the limestone plateau contrast with the silvan beauty of two unspoiled dales on this walk. Monk's Dale is dry. Its river is beneath the limestone pavement but Miller's Dale has a base of impervious clay which holds the water of Derbyshire's River Wye, haunt of trout and river birds.

Wormhill is a little over half way round this walk. It is the birthplace of James Brindley, builder of much of England's canal system. The quiet village makes an ideal stopping place either to explore or perhaps to buy a pot of tea.

Miller's Dale station, once a busy junction where travellers to and from Buxton joined the main line to London, is now a useful car park and forms the northern end of the Monsal Trail.

A The twin viaducts once carried powerful steam locomotives hauling trains on a difficult section of the Midland Line along Monsal Dale. This line, from London St Pancras to Manchester Central, was originally planned to follow an easier route along the Derwent valley through Chatsworth Park to Hathersage. There it was to have joined the Sheffield/Manchester line. By 1849, when the line reached Rowsley near Matlock, the Duke of Devonshire sensed the threat to his beloved Chatsworth and refused the railway company the right of way across his property. Having failed to reach agreement with the duke, the railway company was forced to follow a more difficult route which climbed through Bakewell and then along the steep craggy sides of Monsal Dale. Even this plan was almost spoilt by the Duke of Rutland, who had to be placated by constructing an unnecessary tunnel beneath Haddon Hall and erecting a special station at Bakewell for his use. The saga of ducal autocracy only ended with the erection of a palatial station at rural Hassop, purely for the use of the Duke of Devonshire!

When the railway was first opened, the poet, Ruskin, suggested that it was just another means of exchanging one set of 'fools' for another as locals travelled between Buxton and Bakewell at the expense of the valley.

The Midland Line closed in the 1960s and is now used as the Monsal Trail. This walking trail is from Bakewell to Miller's Dale; tunnels are blocked and bypassed by either existing or concessionary paths but the Miller's Dale and Monsal Head viaducts, so hated by Ruskin, remain open for pedestrian use.

B Monksdale Farm. In the 14th century, there was a small chapel on the site of the farm — hence the name 'Monk's Dale'.

C Viewpoint. Look across the deep trough of Monk's Dale and Miller's Dale to Priestcliffe and the limestone uplands of Taddington Moor.

D Monk's Dale Viewpoint. The special flora and fauna of this densely wooded, narrow rocky dale are protected as part of a nature reserve. Peter Dale to the right, a continuation of Monk's Dale, is not as heavily wooded and more easily accessible.

E Viewpoint. Monk's Dale is to the east, continuing northwards towards Peak Forest as a series of inter-connecting dry dales.

F Wormhill. The quiet upland community will have changed very little since James Brindley, the canal engineer, was born here in 1716. Notice the ancient stocks to one side of the Brindley Memorial and spare a little time to look in on the 700-year-old village church.

G Viewpoint: the rocky buttress of Chee Tor is opposite.

H Viewpoint. Narrow terraces above Blackwell Dale, to the right of the main dale, mark the site of ancient fields. On the left-hand hillside are the remains of an old limestone quarry. The kilns have been preserved as an interesting archaeological feature and can be approached by a track beyond the Miller's Dale viaduct.

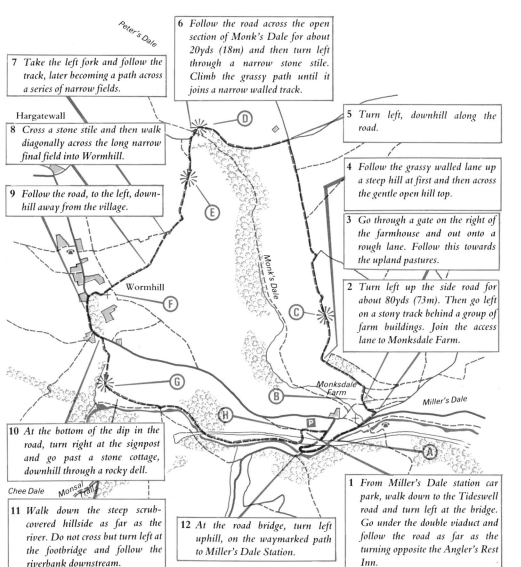

7 Take the left fork and follow the track, later becoming a path across a series of narrow fields.

6 Follow the road across the open section of Monk's Dale for about 20yds (18m) and then turn left through a narrow stone stile. Climb the grassy path until it joins a narrow walled track.

8 Cross a stone stile and then walk diagonally across the long narrow final field into Wormhill.

5 Turn left, downhill along the road.

4 Follow the grassy walled lane up a steep hill at first and then across the gentle open hill top.

9 Follow the road, to the left, down-hill away from the village.

3 Go through a gate on the right of the farmhouse and out onto a rough lane. Follow this towards the upland pastures.

2 Turn left up the side road for about 80yds (73m). Then go left on a stony track behind a group of farm buildings. Join the access lane to Monksdale Farm.

10 At the bottom of the dip in the road, turn right at the signpost and go past a stone cottage, downhill through a rocky dell.

1 From Miller's Dale station car park, walk down to the Tideswell road and turn left at the bridge. Go under the double viaduct and follow the road as far as the turning opposite the Angler's Rest Inn.

11 Walk down the steep scrub-covered hillside as far as the river. Do not cross but turn left at the footbridge and follow the riverbank downstream.

12 At the road bridge, turn left uphill, on the waymarked path to Miller's Dale Station.

25

Walk 11
THOR'S CAVE
4 miles (6.4km) Moderate; one climb of 295ft (90m)

Starting at Wetton, an airy upland village, the walk crosses broad pastures before climbing down through an ancient coral reef into the Manifold Valley. A disused mill at this point is now a welcoming café, well placed for a pause before the steep climb to mysterious Thor's Cave.

6 *Where the farm track turns right, go left following the boundary wall downhill. Move over to the right and then back by an awkward stile in order to avoid an area of dense scrub.*

5 *Turn right, along an access drive and left at its junction with another track.*

4 *Go over the stile in the corner of the field and climb the next to its top boundary. Climb the stile, cross a lane and go through a narrow belt of trees.*

3 *Bear right, away from the wall.*

2 *Go through stiles on either side of a small disused quarry. Follow a faint field path as far as the field boundary below Wetton Hill.*

7 *Continue down the dry valley, through the stockyard at Dale Farm and into the Manifold Valley.*

1 *Park in Wetton and follow the village street past the church. Where the road turns left, follow the direction of the signpost to 'Back of Ecton'.*

8 *Turn left along the valley road, then right and left over the river.*

9 *Go through a gate, away from the road, along the old railway track.*

10 *Turn left, over a footbridge and climb the hillside to Thor's Cave. Take care on the smooth slippery rocks.*

11 *From the front of the cave, follow the concessionary path and walled lane to Wetton.*

Sugarloaf

Wetton Hill

Wettonmill

Darfur Bridge

Thor's Cave

Wetton

A Viewpoint. Butterton church spire rises above the Manifold Valley.

B The prominent knoll to the left of the path is aptly called the Sugarloaf.

C Wetton Mill. Once ground flour for the surrounding villages.

D The valley section of this walk follows part of the route of the Manifold Valley Light Railway, a narrow gauge line which ran between Hulme End and Waterhouses from 1904 to 1934.

E Darfur Bridge. In dry weather, the River Manifold disappears underground at this point, reappearing near Ilam Hall.

F Thor's Cave makes a perfect frame for a breathtaking view of the Manifold Valley.

G Viewpoint. The slender spire of Grindon church stands out across the Manifold.

Walk 12
CARSINGTON PASTURE

6¾ miles (10.9km) Easy/Moderate; two climbs of 333ft (101m) and 200ft (61m)

The small villages of Carsington and Brassington once depended on lead mining for their revenue. The stone cottages housed men who scratched a living below ground to supplement their income from part-time farming. Their small holdings are now incorporated within larger farms and the only tangible remains of mining are humps and hollows dotted along the walk.

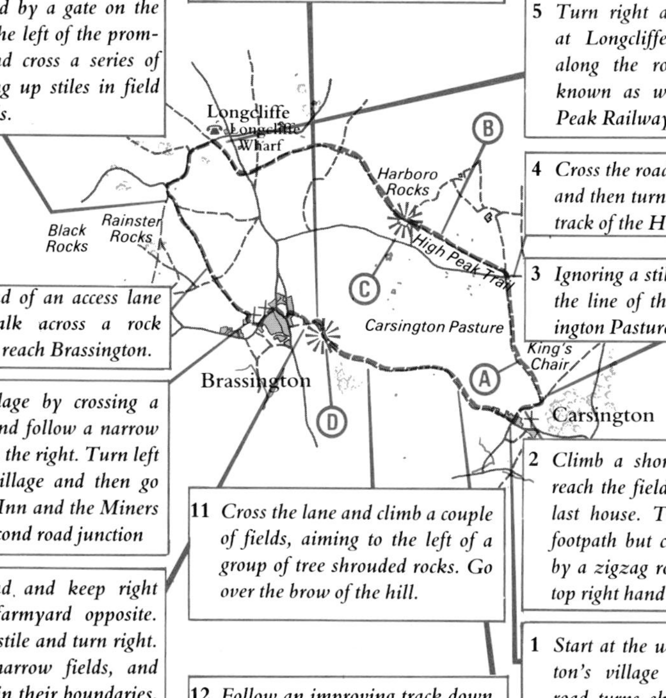

10 *Turn right through a stile and walk round the grassy hillside.*

6 *Leave the road by a gate on the left. Keep to the left of the prominent barn and cross a series of fields by lining up stiles in field boundary walls.*

5 *Turn right away from the trail at Longcliffe Wharf, then left along the road. (Stations were known as wharfs on the High Peak Railway.)*

4 *Cross the road by a couple of stiles and then turn left along the cinder track of the High Peak Trail.*

7 *Cross the head of an access lane and then walk across a rock strewn field to reach Brassington.*

3 *Ignoring a stile, turn left to follow the line of the wall across Carsington Pasture.*

8 *Enter the village by crossing a narrow lane and follow a narrow walled path on the right. Turn left through the village and then go past the Gate Inn and the Miners Arms to the second road junction*

2 *Climb a short flight of steps to reach the field on the right of the last house. There is no obvious footpath but climb the steep field by a zigzag route, aiming for the top right hand corner.*

9 *Cross the road, and keep right through the farmyard opposite. Go through a stile and turn right. Cross three narrow fields, and through stiles in their boundaries. Go left at the last one and climb to the top of the field.*

11 *Cross the lane and climb a couple of fields, aiming to the left of a group of tree shrouded rocks. Go over the brow of the hill.*

12 *Follow an improving track down to Carsington.*

1 *Start at the west end of Carsington's village street. Where the road turns sharp left, turn right along a short lane between groups of cottages.*

Map labels: Longcliffe, Longcliffe Wharf, Harboro Rocks, Black Rocks, Rainster Rocks, High Peak Trail, Carsington Pasture, King's Chair, Brassington, Carsington

A King's Chair is a rough hewn seat carved from a limestone block on the opposite side of the wall. Do not cross as the field is private. The 'chair' looks out over the Henmore valley and the new Carsington Reservoir.

B The High Peak Trail follows the track of the Cromford and High Peak Railway

C Harboro' Rocks and similar outcrops are made from dolomitic or magnesian limestone.

D View of Brassington. 'Branzicton' in the Domesday Book.

Walk 13
HIGH TOR AND THE HEIGHTS OF ABRAHAM
4½ miles (7.2km) Easy

Matlock developed as a spa town during the Victorian era with an enthusiasm which culminated in the construction of the massive Smedley Hydro dominating the northern hillside above the town. The building is now used as the offices of Derbyshire Council. Thermal water still flows but, apart from its use in the indoor swimming pool of the New Bath Hotel, it is largely ignored.

The Victorians fancifully compared the local landscape to Switzerland and this walk certainly has an alpine flavour. There is a cable car system from the foot of High Tor to the summit of the Heights of Abraham. The latter is an attractive area of landscaped woodland high above the Derwent Valley.

Small fees are payable to enter High Tor with its roofless caverns and woodland walks. A fee is also charged for entry to the Heights of Abraham. This covers show caves, other amenities and the cable car. A discount is normally available when embarking on the cable car by showing your copy of this guide.

From the Heights of Abraham, the walk follows a miners' path to Bonsall and its unique market cross. The route returns to Matlock by way of airy Masson Hill.

A Viewpoint. The River Derwent has carved a narrow gorge at the foot of the sheer limestone cliff of High Tor. On the opposite side of the valley, the wooded slopes of the Heights of Abraham lead to Masson Hill. Turn about and allow your eyes to follow the downward slope of High Tor. The hill which rises beyond is composed of gritstone lying on top of the limestone of High Tor. This is Riber Hill, dominated by a curious folly known as Riber Castle. Built in the mid 1800s by John Smedley as a hydropathic hotel, it never flourished, mainly because there was a poor water supply and it fell into disuse in the 1940s.

Today it houses a zoo for rare breeds.

The summit of High Tor has a series of deep roofless caverns which can be explored without a torch.

B If following the alternative route, Matlock Bath's 'Swiss style' station is very much in keeping with the alpine flavour of this walk.

C The Heights of Abraham. This is a convenient refreshment stop. The name commemorates General Wolfe's battle with the French in 1759 to gain control of Canada. The Great Rutland Cavern is nearby. Here you can experience the sights and sounds of a working Derbyshire lead mine in the 17th century. The Victoria Tower is a few yards from the upper cable station and was built as part of a 19th-century 'job creation scheme'. The tower is a good vantage point for viewing the surrounding scenery.

D The pillar of the market cross is mounted on a steep conical plinth which has 10 steps on its uphill side and 13 downhill.

E View of Bonsall village tucked in its hillside cleft.

1 From Matlock, follow the riverside path through Hall Leys Park. Go under the railway bridge as far as a footbridge. Do not cross, but turn left up a narrow lane.

2 Turn right through a gate into the grounds of High Tor. A grassy path leads to the summit café.

3 There are at least three alternative paths from High Tor, including one which follows a narrow ledge across the upper face.

4 Take the cable car to the Heights of Abraham. *Alternative to cable car:* follow the station approach and cross the A6. Climb Upperwood Road opposite as far as the lower entrance to the woodlands.

5 Follow the gravel track for about 40 yds (37m) beyond the upper cable car station and turn left along a level woodland path.

6 At a complex track junction by Ember Farm, bear right towards the farm, then left away from it, along the walled access lane and walk down to Bonsall village.

7 Turn right at the church and follow the road as far as the market cross. The 17th century Kings Head pub is opposite.

8 Follow the walled lane up a steep hill, to the right of the cross. Keep left at the end of the surfaced section to walk along a tree shaded path.

9 Turn right at a 'T' junction. Go through a field gate to follow first a hedge and then a wall on the right.

10 Go through a stone squeezer stile in the right hand wall at the top corner of the field. Cross a small field keeping between two barns.

11 Go through another squeezer stile into a narrow field.

12 Cross the gravel lane and pass through the stile on its opposite side. Keep half right down the grassy hillside on a faint path. Cross ruined walls by stone stiles to be sure of the correct route.

13 Keeping to the right of a boundary hedge, walk downhill through two fields towards the left hand side of Masson Lees Farm.

14 Cross the lane and enter the lower field through an old iron gate. Follow the hedge and cross field boundaries by their stone stiles.

15 Go through a kissing gate at the bottom of the steep field. Climb down the flight of steps at the side of the large house and join the road into Matlock.

Matlock Bridge

Riber Castle (Fauna Reserve)

Masson Lees Farm

High Tor

Masson Hill

Heights of Abraham

Matlock Bath

Bonsall

A B C D

Walk 14
YOULGREAVE AND LATHKILL DALE
8 miles (12.9km) Easy/Moderate

The walk begins in Youlgreave — a village which is linked, albeit historically, with lead mining. Some of the oldest village buildings are still farms and are firmly part of the village structure despite modern development.

Officially, Youlgreave is usually spelt with an 'e' but the locals prefer it as Youlgrave.

Below the village, in quiet Bradford Dale, trout pools originally provided water to power both corn and lead smelt mills. Climbing out of the dale, the walk follows a series of grassy paths across the lush pastures of Calling Low Farm. Gentle breezes blow on the farm, even on the sunniest of days but in winter the story is entirely different. Extensive shelterbelts of trees are planted to break the force of winter gales. Through the trees, one of the finest views across the limestone plateau opens up. Dropping quickly into Cales Dale, the path then leads through the sylvan tranquillity of Lathkill Dale, a dale which was once the scene of intensive mining activity but is now a completely natural valley.

A Opposite the youth hostel, there is a large circular stone water tank. On the dry limestone plateau, obtaining water has been a problem which Youlgreave has overcome by bringing it across Bradford Dale from nearby Stanton Moor. The village is one of the few places with a private water supply. An annual well dressing celebration marks Youlgreave's appreciation for the gift of pure water.

B Middleton-by-Youlgreave stands at the head of Bradford Dale. You can reach it from stage four of the route by turning left instead of right at the main road. One of several Peakland Middletons, this sleepy village was the home of Christopher Fullwood, who raised an army of 1000 lead miners during the Civil War. Thomas Bateman, the 19th century archaeologist, also lived here. Together with teams of local labourers, he dug out large numbers of ancient burial mounds, in a misguided search for treasure.

C The road crosses a tree lined cutting following the line of Long Rake lead vein. Latterly, the Rake has been worked from the surface to extract fluorspar.

D Viewpoint. Lathkill Dale is the wooded ravine to your right and Monyash church spire can be glimpsed in the distance. Directly opposite, across Cales Dale, is One Ash Grange, a prosperous sheep farm, once a monastic penitentiary.

E Natural woodland covering the opposite hillside is part of a nature reserve.

F Stone pillars mark the line of a viaduct which carried water across the dale to Mandale Mine.

G Mandale was one of the largest lead mines in the locality but only the shell of its pit-head gear now remains. **As with all old mines, it is best not to go too close.**

H A notice near the woodland edge lays claim to the private ownership of the path by stating that, on the Thursday of Easter week, anyone using it can be charged one penny.

I Over Haddon is to the left, about ½ mile (0.8km) away by the steep side road. There are several cafés and one pub.

J Youlgreave's historic church is well worth a visit. Look inside at the radiant colours of the east window. The Norman font, with an upside down dragon holding an oil stoup in its mouth, was originally the property of Elton Church. It was thrown out of Elton Church during reconstruction work in Victorian times and found its way to Youlgreave. Inter-village rivalry was only settled when Elton agreed to make do with a copy.

12 Enter private woodland by following a concessionary footpath.

11 Cross the wooden footbridge and turn right, following the riverside path along Lathkill Dale.

13 At the end of the wood, go right, then left around the boundary of a large house. Follow the path along the river bank.

14 On reaching the road, turn right over Conksbury Bridge for about 120yds (110m), then left through a squeezer stile on to a field path. Notices at this point will inform you that teas are on sale at Conksbury Farm 100yds (91m) further up the road.

10 Climb the stile and go steeply down the stepped path into shrubby Cales Dale. Turn right along the dale bottom.

9 Keep left, following signs, through Calling Low farmyard.

15 Follow the field path. Turn right at a narrow lane, past Raper Lodge to reach Youlgreave.

8 Climb the wall stile on the right and cross a series of grassy fields, following occasional waymark posts.

7 Turn left along the road and keep straight on at the junction.

6 Climb the stile on the right and follow a field path uphill as far as the Moor Lane picnic site.

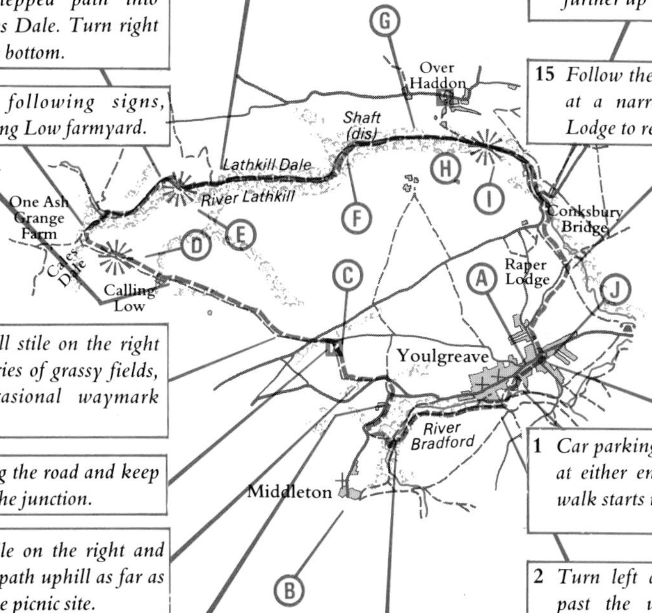

1 Car parking can usually be found at either end of the village. The walk starts in the main street.

2 Turn left down Holywell Lane past the village hall to reach Bradford Dale.

5 Follow the road to the second bend and go left through a stone squeezer stile at the side of a white gate. Cross the field and reach the upper road by a step stile. Ignore the path opposite but turn left to follow the road for about 50yds (46m).

4 Cross the stream by a broad stone bridge on the right, then go left uphill past a ruined mill. Walk beneath trees as far as the road, then turn right.

3 Cross a stone clapper bridge and turn right to follow the riverside path upstream past a series of trout pools.

Map labels: Over Haddon · Shaft (dis) · Lathkill Dale · River Lathkill · One Ash Grange Farm · Cales Dale · Calling Low · Conksbury Bridge · Raper Lodge · Youlgreave · River Bradford · Middleton · G · H · I · F · D · E · C · A · J · B

Walk 15
MONYASH AND FLAGG
8 miles (12.9km) Easy

```
0                              1 mile
|---|---|---|---|---|
0              1 km
```

Monyash developed around the local lead mines. At one time it had a Barmote Court to settle mining disputes and a weekly market which met by a stone cross in front of what is now the Hobbit Inn. Flagg, on the other hand, is a linear village, consisting mostly of farms which rely on the nearby spring for their supplies of water.

5 Cross a grassy strip to reach the road. Turn left through a gate by the 'T' junction. There is no path: follow a diagonal line across the field. Line up gates and stiles to cross a series of narrow fields as far as Rockfield House.

4 Turn left at the track crossroads.

Taddington

3 Cross the road and walk down the cart lane. Ignore waymarked path 8, diverging on the right, and continue uphill along the lane.

Rockfield House

E

2 Go to the right of a shelter belt of trees. Continue to cross boundary walls by their stiles as indicated by the yellow arrows.

Sheldon

6 Keep to the right of the farm. Turn right at the road for about 100yds (91m), then left at a footpath sign. Follow the field path to Flagg, entering the village by way of Hall Farm's stock yard.

F

Hall

D

Flagg

C

1 The Walk starts at the Jack Mere car park in Monyash. Walk northwards, away from the village, to a road junction and turn right for about 50 yds (46m). Cross over a stile on the left (signposted to Taddington) and then pass through a series of meadows.

7 Follow the road away from the village.

Knotlow

8 Leave the road to walk along the farm lane.

G

B

9 Keep to the right of Knotlow Farm, aiming for two prominent ash trees at the top of the field.

Cross

Monyash

A

11 Go left through a squeezer stile and cross the narrow fields by a series of stiles. Enter the village at the side of a row of cottages.

10 Go past a stone barn to the right of an open grassy area and follow the walled lane.

A Jack Mere, now filled in, was one of five artificial pools, or meres, which provided water for the village. Monyash or 'Many ash' appears in the Doomsday Book as 'Maneis'.

B Viewpoint. Look back at the village. The church steeple is the focal point but narrow strip fields, 'fossilised' in their mediev-al system, are all around.

C Strips of mature woodland in the Peak have a dual purpose. They provide a wind break on the exposed upland but their main purpose was to exclude cattle from areas poisoned by lead waste.

D Notice the heather growing on either side of the lane, a rarity in a normally alkaline region.

E Viewpoint of the upper Lath-kill basin with Monyash in the distance and Flagg closer to hand.

F Viewpoint. Flagg, an example of a linear village which de-veloped along a spring line — a rarity on dry limestone uplands.

G From here, there is a good view of Monyash across its 'home' fields.